THE WORLD'S
GREATEST PAINTINGS

THE WORLD'S GREATEST PAINTINGS

Selected Masterpieces
of Famous Art Galleries

EDITED BY
T. LEMAN HARE

ODHAMS PRESS LTD.
LONG ACRE, LONDON, W.C.2

CONTENTS

THE VIGIL

By JOHN PETTIE, R.A.

In the Tate Gallery—British School

John Pettie, R.A.

1839-1893

CHIVALRY, which had as its keynote devotion exercised to the utmost degree, is well personified in this kneeling figure of a handsome acolyte. It was the same spirit, let us remember to his credit, which seized Don Quixote with a noble if misdirected frenzy. Alas, he was two centuries too late for such romance.

John Pettie has shown the young candidate the night before his investiture at vigil, kneeling in front of the high altar of a church. His armour, which according to the rules of knight-errantry he must watch the whole night through, lies at the foot of the altar before him. The symbolic meaning of each piece of armour has been explained to him at the preceding ceremony, and we may call attention to the cruciform sword-hilt, which casts a shadowy crusader's cross on the breast of the youth's mantle.

" The education of the future knight," says Sir Walter Scott in his Essay on Chivalry, " began at an early age." The first step to the order of knighthood was the lowly degree of page, the second that of squire. The honour of knighthood could not be attained till the aspirant was one-and-twenty. In early times, a knight could be created by another knight. Even the highest potentates sought the *accolade*, or stroke which conferred the honour, at the hands of knights of great renown. At length, it became the sole prerogative of sovereigns, as " the true fount of chivalry." Doubtless, John Pettie took his theme from the description of the ritual from Sir Walter. Not until the morrow will the novice in the picture receive the full honour of knighthood. " The candidates watched their arms all night in a church or chapel, and prepared for the honour to be conferred on them by vigil, fast and prayer. They were solemnly divested of the brown frock, which was the appropriate dress of the squire, and, having been bathed, as a symbol of purification of heart, they were attired in the rich garb appropriate to knighthood. They were then solemnly invested with the appropriate arms of a knight."

The next day the novice will be accoutred in his knightly armour, but without helmet, sword, or spurs; a rich mantle will be flung over him and

(Continued)

TWO STRINGS TO HER BOW

By JOHN PETTIE, R.A.

In the Corporation Art Gallery, Glasgow—British School

he will be conducted again to the church with much pomp and ceremony to receive the accolade. His sword will be belted on by the priest, his spurs fastened to his heels, perhaps by ladies of quality, and lastly the oath of chivalry taken " to be loyal to God, the King, and the Ladies."

After the solemnity of " The Vigil," Pettie is deliberately in a playful mood in his " Two Strings to Her Bow." The attractive and self-possessed little lady is clearly bent on mischief. She has a roguish expression, but although she is consciously proud of her conquests she shows favour to neither town buck nor country cousin. Though barely as high as their shoulders, she is complete mistress of the situation. They have just emerged from a shady-sunken lane. How each must have wished the other away. One would say that the more dandified youth might have seized the opportunity of the moment, but not so the other. He is far too shy and too self-conscious. In his perplexity, he cannot walk straight; his hair is ruffled, he clutches his beaver hat nervously, and fingers the edge of his coat. Both are silent, the buck, with the knob of his cane to his lips, is wondering how, by some cunning, he can get rid of his rival.

The time, as indicated by the costume, is 1810; the age of " bucks and bloods," when George, Prince of Wales, afterwards George IV, became Regent.

It is interesting to know that it was owing to the Prince Regent and Beau Brummell that English fashions deprived France of the lead for the first time and became the universal standard of taste for the Continent. In the London Museum is a man's suit of this exact date, cut precisely as seen in this picture. There is a sunny charm about this work, an illustration of manners which is not customary with Pettie. The majority of his pictures deal with the more dramatic moments and sinister aspects of history. He was fond of the glint of armour and weapons and had a great reputation for his treatment of them. Always his preferences were for the costume of bygone days. He was born in Edinburgh, the son of a general merchant, and came to London in 1859. After working for two years as an illustrator, he abandoned its practice and speedily became popular, through his " Drum-Head Court Martial," which was exhibited in the Royal Academy. In 1866 Pettie was elected to the Royal Academy as an Associate, and in 1874 he became a full member.

A BOY WITH A RABBIT

By SIR HENRY RAEBURN, R.A., R.S.A.

In the Diploma Gallery, Burlington House—British School

Sir Henry Raeburn, R.A., R.S.A.

1756-1823

AS a portrait painter, Raeburn takes a high place among artists who specialised in this form. If he has not the depth and tenderness of Rembrandt, or the scholarly, analytical power of Leonardo, he still has a fine sense of character and the ability to illuminate a feature and accentuate a manner.

He was fortunate in living at a time before costume was standardised, before mankind was shorn of those " fine feathers " that were part of the sheer joy of portrait painting. In the eighteenth century there were no photographs to dull the edge of pictorial appreciation, and if one wanted one's effigy to hand down to posterity, none could fill a space in an ancestral hall better than Master Raeburn, of Edinburgh. He knew his craft, and a glorious one it was, dignified eventually by a knighthood and the grand title of King's Limner for Scotland. Raeburn was born at Stockbridge, Edinburgh, in 1756, eleven years after the Jacobite Rebellion. His father, Robert Raeburn, a mill owner, came of good old Border stock : the lad was left early an orphan and his elder brother, though himself only sixteen, fathered him and sent him to the famous school of Heriot's Hospital, where the boy received such careful training that his good manners were a life-long asset. He was apprenticed to a goldsmith, but, feeling that his destiny was for a larger medium, he began to paint early in life, and soon came into favour.

His marriage at the age of 22 to the widow of Count Leslie, a lady of some means, helped his art education by making it possible for him to study for two years in Rome. On his return he soon became the foremost portrait painter in the north, and, in spite of his immense output, kept his art at a very high level of excellence. Raeburn was equally successful in his portraits of beautiful women and children and the one reproduced here— " A Boy with a Rabbit," his diploma work for the Royal Academy—is among his best things. It is a portrait of Raeburn's godson and favourite step-grandson, Henry Raeburn Inglis, a very popular picture, which is at the Diploma Gallery. Raeburn died in 1823 after a life of continuous success.

THE ANSIDEI MADONNA

By RAPHAEL SANZIO

In the National Gallery—Umbrian School

Raphael Sanzio
1483-1520

IT would be difficult to think of a name in the whole realm of pictorial art that would evoke more instantly pleasant recollections in the mind of the ordinary man or woman than that of the great Umbrian painter, Raphael, who was born at Urbino on April 6, 1483.

His father, Giovanni Santi, appears to have been also a painter and no mean poet, and was engaged at the court of Guidobaldo, Duke of Urbino. There is little doubt that the young painter inherited his rare good looks from his mother, Magia Ciarla, a famous beauty and a woman of great endowments, and that she was his inspiration for many of his famous Madonnas. Both his parents died while he was still a lad, but even at this early age, no doubt from the influence of his father, he had decided upon his career.

The colour plate here reproduced, one of Raphael's masterpieces, known as " The Ansidei Madonna," is one of the most precious possessions of the National Gallery and was painted about 1506. The Madonna and Child are shown attended by St. John the Baptist and St. Nicholas of Bari. This picture was painted for the private chapel of Filipo di Simone Ansidei, from whom it takes its name. Eventually the picture passed into the possession of the third Duke of Marlborough, and in 1884 it became known that the eighth Duke was thinking of selling his collection. A great effort was made by the Government to secure Raphael's masterpiece for the nation and it was ultimately secured by Mr. Gladstone, then Chancellor of the Exchequer, for the sum of £70,000.

At the age of twenty-five, in 1508, Raphael was called to Rome by Pope Julius II, there to meet his great rival, Michelangelo. Raphael had the advantage over the gruff, brusque Michelangelo, and soon became the favourite of their patron, honours being showered on him.

Raphael was now rich and powerful and even contemplated a marriage with the niece of Cardinal Bibbiena, but while painting " The Transfiguration," now in St. Peter's, he caught malaria and died on April 6, 1520, at the age of thirty-seven; and the picture was finished later by Giulio Romano.

THE SYNDICS

By REMBRANDT VAN RYN

In the Ryksmuseum, Amsterdam—Dutch School

Rembrandt Van Ryn
1606-1669

REMBRANDT—whose great name has a universal significance, and whose art, it has been well said, is not for an age, but for all time—was, undoubtedly, the greatest of Dutch masters; and it is, therefore, hardly believable that, up to seventy years ago, his alleged loose habits eclipsed his genius and caused him to be much neglected, even John Ruskin allowing himself to say that " the aim of Rembrandt was to paint the foulest things he could see—by rushlight ! "

Rembrandt was born at Leyden on July 15, 1606, the son of a miller, Harmen Gerritszoon Van Ryn; his mother being a baker's daughter, Cornelia Williemsdochter. His father, well-to-do and ambitious for his son, instead of keeping him in his business like his three elder brothers, sent him, when fourteen, to study law at the Leyden University; but after a period there the boy shattered all his father's dreams by electing to be a painter. His disappointed father apprenticed him to Jacob Van Swanenburgh. He also worked at Amsterdam with Pieter Lastman, but neither of these masters had any real influence upon the strong individuality of their pupil.

Rembrandt left Leyden in 1631 for Amsterdam, where most of his patrons resided. He lodged there with a friend, Hendrick Van Uylenborch, of an aristocratic Dutch family, who had given up painting for art dealing, and whose cousin, Saskia, Rembrandt married in 1634. This marriage enabled him—at least for a time—to become independent of demands made upon him by his patrons that they should be portrayed in the stiff and conventional way which was then in vogue.

Saskia died in 1642, after a few years of happy married life. Rembrandt's admiration for his young wife is clearly seen in the many portraits and studies of her which he made during these eight short years. Dresden has the famous " Saskia in a Hat," also " Rembrandt and Saskia "; the Hermitage at Leningrad possesses Saskia as " Flora "; and at Cassel there is the half-length " Saskia in Profile," holding a bunch of rosemary, the Dutch sign of betrothal; all of them superb canvases, all of them of his best period.

(Continued)

MAN IN ARMOUR

By REMBRANDT VAN RYN

In the National Gallery of Scotland, Edinburgh—Dutch School

And now pupils clamoured at the door of his studio. Rembrandt employed them little on his works, but set each one in a separate cell so that they should not influence one another, but each keep his own individuality.

Prominent among these pupils were such well-known names as Ferdinand Bol, his fellow pupil, Govert Flinck, and the famous landscape painter, Philips Koninck, whose works are often passed off as those of the master, in spite of the fact that in his lifetime they rarely touched his paintings.

His working day was sacred to his art, and he permitted no one, however exalted in rank, to interfere with his labours or to waste his time. Patrician society did not interest him, and all his sympathies were with the workers. He was content with his home and a few close friends, and he did not join any of the many guilds and associations available to artists.

It is likely that this aloofness, added to his extravagance, contributed largely to the clouds which, in the year 1654, began to gather round him, as well as his uncompromising behaviour and his rebellion against the conventionalities of his time. Matters were not improved by his relations with Hendrickje Stoffels, which caused considerable scandal; on the other hand, it seems clear that this lady, whom he married later, was a loyal helpmate to Rembrandt, and did everything in her power to save the situation. At last, in 1656, Rembrandt became bankrupt; a seizure was made of his pictures and household goods and the sale of his treasures realized an insignificant sum. Shortly afterwards, his house was sold and the great painter found himself homeless. In spite of these adversities, and oncoming blindness, he continued to work hard for a further twelve years almost to the day of his death, which occurred on October 8, 1669. It is no easy matter in the case of a genius like Rembrandt to select two representative pictures for reproduction, for his output was so large and varied. It was in 1661 that Rembrandt painted a great work for the Guild of Drapers, called " The Syndics of the Cloth Hall," now in the Ryksmuseum, at Amsterdam, here reproduced. There was a demand for such important groups at that time, and both Frans Hals and Rembrandt surpassed themselves in the production of them. It is more than likely that this noble work, like many another, by the same artist, was thought little of in his own day. Our second plate is a magnificent study of a warrior in armour, which is in the National Gallery of Scotland.

AGE OF INNOCENCE

By SIR JOSHUA REYNOLDS, P.R.A.

In the National Gallery—British School

Sir Joshua Reynolds, P.R.A.
1723-1792

SIR JOSHUA REYNOLDS, the first President of the Royal Academy which he was largely instrumental in founding, was born at Plymton Earl on July 16, 1723. His father, Samuel Reynolds, being the headmaster of the local grammar school. Some idea of this beautiful spot in Devonshire may be obtained by glancing at Turner's famous "Crossing the Brook." In 1740, when seventeen, young Reynolds was sent to London to the studio of Thomas Hudson, also a Devonian. It was not long before Hudson, being jealous of his pupil, found a pretext for dismissing him, whereupon Reynolds set up as a portrait painter in Plymouth.

Three years spent later in Italy, in studying the old masters, contributed much to his development. On his return to London, he became the leading portrait painter and succeeded Allan Ramsay as Painter in Ordinary to George III. From 1760 to the date of his death, Reynolds resided in the well-known house on the west side of Leicester Square, where he painted many of his most famous masterpieces.

For many years the chief rival to Reynolds was Thomas Gainsborough, but it is to the credit of these two men of genius that the School of British painting was rescued from a somewhat low standard and became, after a long period of foreign influences, more definitely English in its characteristics.

Reynolds delighted in painting children and, in his hands, they remained children. The typically English portrait, " Age of Innocence," which is the subject of our reproduction here, has a never-failing appeal to visitors to the National Gallery and has been engraved since it was painted in 1788 in many styles and sizes. The child is said to have been the artist's grand-niece, Theophilia Gwatkin. Reynolds' liking for society was useful to him : he was very sociable, went to entertainments, and loved the theatre.

On July 13, 1790, Reynolds was painting the portrait of a child when blindness afflicted his left eye : he knew then that his painting days were over and wrote to Sheridan, " There is now an end of the pursuit; the race is over whether it is lost or won." He became quite blind before he died.

MONNA POMONA

By DANTE GABRIEL ROSSETTI

In the Tate Gallery—British School

Dante Gabriel Rossetti
1828—1882

THERE is a poetical quality about this picture, which is typical of Rossetti's vision. He was something of a dreamer, and founded his work more upon art than on life.

Born into an age of increasing industrialism, this poet-painter encouraged a tendency to look back to the ages of faith and chivalry. His pictures and poetry are frequently inspired by sacred themes, legends, and history. He was the son of the Italian patriot and refugee, Gabriel Rossetti, and was born at Charlotte Street, Portland Place, in 1828. Coming under the influence of Holman Hunt and Ford Madox Brown, Rossetti helped to found the Pre-Raphaelite movement, of which the youthful Millais was also a member. He painted a large number of pictures in oil and water-colours, many of which eventually found their way into public galleries. Some of them, in reproduction, find a place in thousands of homes. " The Meeting of Dante and Beatrice," " Dante's Dream," and " Beata Beatrix " satisfy a need for romance in a modern world.

Rossetti married Elizabeth Siddal, a beautiful milliner. She was a woman of considerable talent, was encouraged by her husband and Ruskin to learn to draw, and thus became a helpful critic of her husband's work. When she died, Rossetti placed in her coffin the manuscripts of his early poems, but was permitted to recover them some years later.

As a poet he is famous for " The Blessed Damozel," a mystical ecstasy, and a sequence of technically perfect sonnets called the " House of Life." For some time he lived at 16 Cheyne Walk, his house being a museum of rare and curious antiquities and a meeting place for artists and poets. Rossetti was a man of genius, equally at home with painting and literature; but a study of his works will make it clear that this Italian-born artist was never interested in the life of England which went on around him.

After a strenuous life in which worldly success, difficulties, quarrels and controversy were mingled, Rossetti lost his health, was stricken with paralysis, and died at Birchington-on-Sea at the comparatively early age of 54.

LE CHAPEAU DE PAILLE

By SIR PETER PAUL RUBENS

In the National Gallery—Flemish School

Sir Peter Paul Rubens

1577 - 1640

BORN at Siegen on the eve of the feast of Ss. Peter and Paul, this famous painter became known as Peter Paul Rubens. His father, a rather obscure magistrate, but of boundless ambition, had in early life married a lady of fine character named Maria Pypelincks.

Young Rubens was the natural courtier his father had vainly aspired to become; he spoke several languages and was a witty and cultured man. The Italian tour being considered a necessary part of an artist's upbringing, Rubens found his way, at twenty-three, to Italy, where he became the friend of Gonzaga, Duke of Mantua, who made him his court painter.

Having returned in 1609 to his native country, Rubens settled in Antwerp and, in the same year, married his first wife, Isabella Brant, a lady whom he immortalised in many portraits and several religious pictures. It was in 1610 that Rubens painted his magnificent " Elevation of the Cross," now in Antwerp Cathedral; he was soon in great demand and gathered around him an army of pupils and assistants. He built an enormous house containing a large workshop for their accommodation and his home became a kind of art factory to which orders came pouring in, so that for twenty years he was rich and prosperous.

In the year 1626, Rubens suffered the great loss of his wife, possibly from the plague, which was then raging in Antwerp. For some years after his wife's death he was engaged in various diplomatic missions in France and Spain and in 1630 he was in England, where he painted many portraits of famous people; and, before leaving this country, the King knighted him for bringing about the political peace between England and Spain. On December 30, 1630, Rubens married Helen Fourment, a cousin of his first wife, and it was a sister, Suzanna Fourment, who sat for him for his famous painting, " Le Chapeau de Paille," here reproduced, one of the artist's great masterpieces now in the National Gallery. Seven other portraits of her are in existence. For many years Rubens was crippled with gout, and he died on May 30, 1640, a great artist, a devoted husband, a faithful friend, and a generous rival.

THE PARSON'S DAUGHTER

By GEORGE ROMNEY

In the National Gallery—British School

George Romney
1734-1802

THIS great portrait painter of the eighteenth century was one of the three reigning masters of the period, his rivals being Sir Joshua Reynolds and Thomas Gainsborough, both however his seniors. It was on his arrival in London that George Romney adopted a new spelling for his name for, until then, he used his father's name which was Rumney—a man of gipsy blood of the Border country, to whom George Romney was born in 1734. The lad was apprenticed to a wandering portrait painter, of spendthrift habits, Christopher Steele.

It was during this apprenticeship that Romney fell ill and was attended by the daughter of his landlady, Mary Abbot, whom he married in 1756. This was an unfortunate alliance for, although his wife was always good and loyal to him, Romney appears to have been shy of introducing his humble partner to his rich patrons, and on starting for London in March, 1762, he left her in Kendal.

George Romney was a man of reserved shy disposition, never too sure of himself and generous to a fault and it can be imagined what a change was brought about in his life when there suddenly appeared in his studio the famous Emma Hart, who afterwards became Lady Hamilton. She was from the artistic point of view such an inspiration to the indefatigable painter that he produced one masterpiece after another in which he represented the beautiful Emma in a variety of characters.

The subject of our colour plate, " The Parson's Daughter," was acquired for the National Gallery in 1879 : it is not known for certain whom the lady represents, but in all probability it is Miss Elizabeth Close, whose portrait, as Mrs. Mark Currie, is also in the National Gallery.

The last few years of Romney's life were clouded by mental derangement, during which he was obsessed with the desire to produce enormous allegorical pictures. It was during this time that he bethought himself of his wife, now elderly, who had waited for him in the North for thirty-seven years. She did her best to calm his deranged mind and watched over him for the rest of his days. He died on the 15th of November, 1802, hopelessly insane.

OFF VALPARAISO

By THOMAS JAQUES SOMERSCALES

In the Tate Gallery—British School

Thomas Jaques Somerscales
1842-1928

A GALLANT sight is such a clipper as this in full sail on a breezy morning, catching the rosy light as she ploughs the waves. It is below the line, in the southern seas, and we can make out from the direction of the sun's light that she is setting her course northwards. The brightly dressed crew in the shore boat is being hailed from her foredeck, whilst, aloft, some of her own crew are taking in sail. To the left is the low-lying coast of Chili, the extreme edge of the Cordilleras de los Andes. Crisped foam flakes here and there from the dark blue rolling waters, and in the foreground is a solitary seagull. There is a sense of tropical heat and in the sky some suggestion of approaching storm.

When this picture appeared on the Royal Academy walls in 1899 it created something of a sensation. The depth and volume of the heaving water, the feeling of air and space and the searing sub-tropical wind that blows alternately hot and cold, proclaimed it as one of the most intensely realistic renderings of the sea that had been seen for many years.

In the torrid clime
Dark-heaving, boundless, endless, and sublime,

Somerscales' knowledge of the sea was almost born in him. That he is familiar with every detail of a sailing vessel is clearly evident in this fine rendering of an iron four-master. His father was a shipmaster, whose headquarters were at Hull, where he was born. He became a naval schoolmaster and worked for some time in this capacity until he took up painting in both oil and water-colour. Although he had reached the age of fifty-seven when he painted the picture " Off Valparaiso," little had been heard of him previously, but henceforth his reputation was secure.

This first success, the forerunner of many others, perhaps caused him to cling rather closely to a given line of subjects. The picture was purchased for the nation by the trustees of the Chantrey Bequest ; it forms part of the Tate Gallery collection and being much in demand is often lent elsewhere.

CARNATION, LILY, LILY, ROSE

By JOHN SINGER SARGENT, R.A.

In the Tate Gallery—British School

John Singer Sargent, R.A.
1856-1925

MANY and curious are the stories relating to famous pictures, but none is more amusing or appealing than the facts about the creation of " Carnation, Lily, Lily, Rose."

It was in 1885 that Sargent saw a summer-evening effect of Chinese lanterns hung among lilies in a garden at Pangbourne. That year he went to stay with some friends at Broadway, in Gloucestershire; the scene so haunted his imagination that he induced one of these friends, Mrs. Barnard, to allow her two little daughters to pose for him in a garden at Broadway. According to Sir Edmund Gosse, whose letter describing the incident is printed in the Hon. Evan Charteris' " Life of Sargent," the twilight effect was so fleeting that Sargent could paint only for a few minutes, but working every day the picture took shape, and became the talk of the neighbourhood.

The weeks passed, the summer flowers faded and died, and artificial ones were obtained from London. As the evenings grew colder, the young models were dressed in long sweaters, over which their white dresses were pulled. Sargent muffled himself up like an arctic explorer. The picture remained unfinished that year. The artist, however, returned to the place and subject the following summer, and the little girls, though a year older, were willing collaborators in the great work. When, at last, their united efforts came to a conclusion, there was still the question of the title to solve. It happened that a member of the party had sung a song in which the lines " Carnation, Lily, Lily, Rose " appeared. Humming the tune to himself, Sargent remembered the line, and decided to use it for his picture.

" Carnation, Lily, Lily, Rose " is an example of the immense pains that Sargent always took, however well he was able to hide them in the final result.

The most successful portrait painter of his time, he was born in Florence, studied in Paris, and worked mostly in London and America. His best-known portraits are the Ellen Terry as Lady Macbeth, at the Tate Gallery, the superb full-length of Lord Ribbesdale and the group of portraits of the Wertheimer family. He became a member of the Royal Academy in 1897.

THE LETTER

By GERARD TER BORCH

In the Mauritshuis, The Hague—Dutch School

Gerard Ter Borch
1617-1681

IN the year 1617, there was living at Zwolle, in Holland, a man of the name of Ter Borch, who made a fair competence by combining the rare callings of a tax-collector and painter. This man was the father of the renowned Dutch master, Gerard Ter Borch, who was born in the same year. Ter Borch the elder, being himself no mean practitioner of the Arts, was able to appreciate his son's talents at an early age and gave him every encouragement, thus avoiding the early struggles of the young painter.

Young Ter Borch, at the age of 15 in 1632, was sent by his father to Amsterdam to study with one of the leading portrait-painters; within two years he had surpassed his master. In 1634, he went to Haarlem as a pupil to Philip Molyn, but he was by this time so accomplished in his art that his master painted in collaboration with him.

It is well known that the Dutch school of painters of the seventeenth century was chiefly famous for its beautiful rendering of the people of the upper middle class with their delightful home surroundings, but Gerard Ter Borch was to become more especially a painter of more aristocratic types of people and their circles. It is therefore not surprising to learn that about the year 1635 he found himself in England, where he came under the influence of Van Dyck. He also learnt much of the technique of Velasquez, for he paid a visit to Spain shortly afterwards. Ter Borch was one of the many painters whose keen observation enabled them to borrow ideas and methods from other masters, while being gifted also with the power of developing an individual style which could legitimately absorb that which was acquired from others.

We illustrate here " The Letter," a portrait of a lady, which is also a most elegant and refined work of art and one of the treasures of the Art Gallery at the Hague. This genius of the Dutch school, more fortunate than many others of the century, never suffered poverty nor neglect : he died in his 64th year and was buried in the family vault in his native town.

BACCHUS AND ARIADNE

By TITIAN VECELLIO

In the National Gallery—Venetian School

Titian Vecellio
1486-1576

WE come now to one of the names in Italian art which is univers-
ally known and esteemed not only by artists but also by all
educated people. In some respects he shares this world-wide
admiration with Raphael and Michelangelo, but for different reasons. In
any case, it may be truly said of all three of these artists that the general
public and the art world are more or less agreed about them.

Titian Vecellio, unlike his great master, Bellini, was not primarily
a religious painter (often far from it), although he did paint, in the course
of his long career, many beautiful and famous pictures of religious subjects,
but without that intense spirit of devotion which was so marked a feature
of the work of Bellini and many of the Italian primitives.

Titian was born at Pievi di Cadore, to the north of Venice—he was the
second son of Gregorio Vecellio, of an old and respected Venetian family.
At an early age he was sent to Venice to study painting, to Giovanni Bellini,
where he met Giorgione, who, although twelve years his senior, exerted a
deep impression on the youth and greatly influenced his outlook on Art. The
plague of 1510, which swept Venice, took Giorgione; and, after the death of
his friend, Titian went to Padua, but, dissatisfied there, he returned to settle
in Venice, where he was soon the leading painter. Hotly opposed by Bellini
and Carpaccio, he applied for the office of Official Painter to the State,
which he obtained only after the death of his old master, three years later.

The magnificent painting called "Bacchus and Ariadne" (here reproduced) was painted about 1520 for the Duke Federigo Gonzaga. It is
one of Titian's undoubted masterpieces and stands unrivalled among the
Italian pictures in the National Gallery. The subject is not only of Pagan
origin, but seems to be obviously painted from a purely physical and
material point of view. Bacchus is here seen springing from his chariot
to greet Ariadne, daughter of Minos, King of Crete, who has just been
deserted by Theseus. In the distance can be seen the white sails of the
departing ships of Theseus; a train of nymphs, satyrs, and fauns, returning

(Continued)

FLORA

By TITIAN VECELLIO

In the Uffizi Gallery, Florence—Venetian School

from a sacrifice, escort Bacchus. The picture was bought for the National Gallery in 1826.

Speaking generally, it may be said that the very name Titian is synonymous in most minds with that sumptuous colour for which Venice became justly renowned, although it can hardly be seriously held that Titian was more gifted in this respect than many of his fellow citizens. It must be remembered that the very position of Venice herself upon the lagoons, at the head of the Adriatic, with the comings and goings of merchants and shipping from every land, gave unrivalled opportunities for the appreciation and study of colour; added to this were the enormous prosperity of the city and the inborn love of pageantry in the people, which was freely indulged on every possible occasion. The consequence was that the painters of Venice used bright colours owing to an instinctive love of them, and not, as the Florentine masters did, merely as a pleasant addition to their scholarly compositions.

Our second colour plate, "Flora," in the great Florentine Gallery the Uffizi, may not be literally a portrait, but is most likely a study of the artist's vision of ideal feminine beauty. Although an early work, one feels that Titian has in this superb picture left to future generations a type of Venetian womanhood which few people, whether versed in the arts or not, can fail to admire. In spite of our progress in many fields, it would be no easy task to find in Europe to-day an artist capable of producing a work so typical of his time as this painting is of sixteenth-century Venice. Titian was among the greatest of portrait painters. Visitors to the great Italian Exhibition in London in 1930 will remember the stately portrait of a lady called " La Bella " from the Pitti Gallery, Florence, and also the wonderful study of an old man which represented Pope Paul III, from the Naples Museum. Several great portraits by this famous artist are in the Uffizi Gallery, notably those of the Duke and Duchess of Urbino, and our National Gallery also possesses a portrait by Titian said to be of Ariosto. Like many outstanding masters who survived to a great age, Titian during his latter years produced some of his greatest works, though it is of interest to note that in some of his most beautiful portraits of his late period, such as the self-portrait in the Prado of Madrid, he relied more on quiet schemes of lovely grey harmonies than on brilliant colour. He died suddenly of the plague on August 27, 1576.

CROSSING THE BROOK

By JOSEPH MALLORD WILLIAM TURNER, R.A.

In the National Gallery—British School

Joseph Mallord William Turner, R.A.
1775 - 1851

IN dingy Maiden Lane, at No. 26, long since pulled down, there lived a William Turner—a barber, and his wife, Mary Marshall, to whom was born on St. George's Day, April 23, 1775, a son whom they christened Joseph Mallord William Turner, and who was destined to become one of the greatest painters of modern times.

In the National Gallery there hangs a self-portrait, somewhat flattering, of a pretty youth, full face, large eyes, heavy nose and drooping under lips, painted at the age of 15. From his mother, a woman of furious temper, Turner only inherited his short stature. From his father, a covetous but kindly man, he doubtless acquired his industry and his weakness for " economy." "Dad taught me nothing," said he, "except to save half-pence ! " This he certainly did on many amusing occasions.

After Mrs. Turner's death the old man lived with his son for the rest of his life and, in spite of his somewhat tyrannical rule, Turner loved him sincerely. But no human being or other interest ever interfered with his art, which to him was life itself.

At nine Turner went to school at New Brentford, but he was hopeless, drawing always and anywhere instead of learning, and indeed he remained practically illiterate all his life. In a publication called " Coast Scenery," Mr. Coombes complained that " Turner's compositions were so extra-ordinary as to be unintelligible ! " In spite of his father's parsimony, he was apprenticed to the architect Hardwick, during which period he studied painting in his spare time. He worked incessantly with various masters, one of whom was Sir Joshua Reynolds, saving his money, and in 1814, with his father's financial help, he bought a house at Twickenham. Many stories are told of his father's comical attempts to add to the area of the property by encroaching little by little upon the roadway, much to the anger of the authorities.

Ambition was strong in him. Of a secretive nature, he kept much to himself; at most times very mean, yet capable of great kindnesses and

(Continued)

THE FIGHTING TÉMÉRAIRE

By JOSEPH MALLORD WILLIAM TURNER, R.A.

In the National Gallery—British School

sacrifices; capricious too, as the mood of the moment usually governed his actions. Late in life, he hoarded his pictures, even buying them when they came up for sale at Christie's.

In 1830, at the age of 55, he lost his father. Left alone his habits grew very slovenly and he became more of a misanthrope. In his seventy-second year he disappeared suddenly, turning up on varnishing days at the Royal Academy. None knew where he lived until his faithful servant, Hannah Danby, discovered by chance that he was living at Cremorne Cottage, in Chelsea, as a Mr. Booth. On this information, Mr. Harper, his trustee, went there only to find the artist dying.

Wheeled to the window in his chair, and propped up on pillows, he took a last look at the river and his beloved sun, and died, his last words being " The Sun is God."

Turner made a life-long study of the effects of light and was probably the only painter up to his day who fearlessly looked into the face of the sun, whether in its rising or setting, and dared to paint pictures of what he saw—sometimes even what he hoped he saw. Constable generously called them his " Golden Visions." The wondrous series of landscapes, now in a special room of the Tate Gallery, represents the best and greatest phase of Turner's colossal achievement when he bursts forth as the true pioneer of modern art.

One of his most famous masterpieces is " Crossing the Brook," now in the National Gallery and here reproduced. It was painted in the year 1815. This lovely landscape is taken from near the Morwell Rocks looking south-wards in the direction of Plymouth, although, as in many other pictures, he made no claim to exact topographical rendering.

Our second illustration "Fighting Téméraire" is one of the artist's best-known and most admired works and was first exhibited at the Royal Academy in 1839. It may be of interest to note the way in which his masterpiece came to be painted. In the year 1838, when Turner was travelling to Green-wich by water with some friends they happened to pass a steam-tug with an old battleship in tow. " That is a fine subject for you, Turner," remarked one of the party. Turner acting upon his advice painted the " Fighting Téméraire tugged to her last berth to be broken up "—his original title.

PORTRAIT OF VAN DER GEEST

By SIR ANTHONY VAN DYCK

In the National Gallery—Flemish School

Sir Anthony Van Dyck
1599-1641

IN the throng of pupils of the Rubens studio, or factory, one emerged whose name was to become a household word—Van Dyck. He was born on March 22, 1599, at Antwerp, where his father, Frans Van Dyck, was a prosperous merchant. When ten years of age, Van Dyck joined the Guild of St. Luke as pupil to Hendrick Van Balen; at sixteen, he went to the studio of Rubens and before he was twenty became his assistant. Rubens was of so large and generous a nature that by the time his young pupil came of age he was already famous. It was at the age of twenty years that Anthony Van Dyck painted the astonishing portrait of Cornelius Van der Geest, in the National Gallery, one of our colour plates. The dignity of pose and vital characteristics of this portrait were so marked that it is small wonder that for a long time it was supposed to be a work by Rubens himself.

In 1621, Van Dyck left for Italy on the advice of Rubens; and, after travelling round the country studying the work of the great Italian masters, he settled at Genoa. This was a period in which he was to produce some of his most famous masterpieces in portraiture which are so much sought for by collectors.

During his residence in Italy, Van Dyck compiled a sketch-book, which is now a much-prized treasure in the Duke of Devonshire's collection at Chatsworth. The Genoa period produced two famous portraits, now in the National Gallery, of the Marquess and Marchioness Cattanio, which were acquired for about £13,000 each.

Van Dyck returned to his native Antwerp in 1628, and about the year 1631 he painted the superb pair of portraits now in the Wallace Collection of Philippe le Roy and his wife.

In 1632, Van Dyck made his second visit to London—he had already worked there for a time for James I—this time at the invitation of Charles I, who found him a house in Blackfriars, appointed him " Principalle Paynter in Ordinary to their Majesties," and duly knighted him. He was also provided with a country house at Eltham, in Kent, together with a

(Continued)

CHARLES I

By SIR ANTHONY VAN DYCK

In the Louvre—Flemish School

fixed salary and was to be paid in addition for each painting produced.

With the exception of one brief visit to Antwerp, which lasted twelve months, Van Dyck passed the remainder of his life in England, where he was kept busy painting that series of portraits which made his name so famous. One of these portraits was that of Philip Lord Wharton, as a Shepherd boy, which passed later to the Empress Catherine of Russia.

Many of Van Dyck's finest portraits may be seen at Windsor Castle, and there is hardly a great mansion in this country dating from the seventeenth century which does not possess one or more portrait masterpieces by him. Although it may be admitted that the period in which Van Dyck worked gave him great opportunities, owing to the splendour of the costumes then worn, together with architectural surroundings, nevertheless he stands out as the greatest portrait painter of the aristocratic type in the history of painting.

Owing to his position as court painter, it became the duty of the master to paint the King and his Queen, Henrietta Maria, which he did many times. There is one fine portrait of the King in the National Gallery and another at Buckingham Palace; but the one we reproduce is undoubtedly his great masterpiece in this line, being the portrait of Charles I in the Musée du Louvre, in Paris. This is a most dignified composition in which we see the King standing beside his horse which is being held by the Marquess of Hamilton, who is in attendance on the King.

It may be imagined that Van Dyck lived in magnificent style, having no real financial troubles; but, although his income was enormous, he spent it very freely. It was at the suggestion of the King, who reproved him for his extravagance, that in 1639 the artist married Mary Ruthven, who was related to the Royal family, and whom he naturally painted on several occasions; the most notable portrait of her being that in the Munich Gallery.

Being much sought after and spoilt by rich and powerful clients, Van Dyck took part in every kind of exhausting pleasure, in consequence of which he became, towards the end of his life, inclined to treat his great calling too much as a money-making concern, for which purpose he employed a small army of assistants who prepared and started his pictures for him. It was towards the end of 1641 during a visit to Paris that the health of Van Dyck failed. He hastened back to Blackfriars where, on December 8, he died.

THE VIRGIN AND CHILD AND DONOR

By JAN VAN EYCK

In the Louvre—Flemish School

Jan Van Eyck
1385-1441

THE name Van Eyck is one of the most renowned and glorious in the history of art. It may be that there was only one Van Eyck, his name being Jan. A cloud of falsity and legend has grown up around the name Hubert, and his very existence is now being disputed. But with Jan we are on safe ground. From 1422 there is fairly complete documentary evidence. In 1421 he entered the service of John of Bavaria at the Hague as court painter and " valet de chambre " at five and fourpence a day, and in May, 1425, he was taken over in like capacity by Philip the Good, Duke of Burgundy, at a salary of 100 lires.

Jan Van Eyck was an active and busy traveller, being employed upon several missions, and in 1428 he joined Philip's embassy to Lisbon to paint the portrait of Infanta Isabella, the result of which decided the Duke's choice of a bride. Storms and gales delayed the voyage so that the vessel was compelled to seek refuge in England to refit.

In 1433, Jan married Margaret, presumed to be the sister-in-law of John Arnolfini, whose portrait together with his wife he painted in 1434.

Popular tradition has assigned to the Van Eyck brotherhood the invention of oil painting. This view cannot be strictly upheld, but certain it is that Van Eyck vastly improved upon all known methods by clarifying oils and varnishes and by particular care in the preparation of pigments. As an illustrator of ideas, Jan may be credited as the founder of the easel picture tradition. Suddenly the primitive view of painting and the conventional repetition of forms fell behind, and with Van Eyck, as Professor Alec Faure has said, came " the flowering of Gothic art, whose expression in colour had ripened little by little in the pages of the missels." The picture by which Jan Van Eyck is here represented is the magnificent group in the Louvre, " The Virgin and Child and Donor." On the right the Madonna is seen being crowned by an angel, whilst on the left is the figure of Rollin, the Chancellor of Philip the Good, adoring the Christ child; the centre is devoted to a wonderful landscape with an enchanting distant view.

PHILIP IV

By DIEGO DE SILVA Y VELAZQUEZ

In the National Gallery—Spanish School

Diego de Silva y Velazquez
1599-1660

VELAZQUEZ, the great Spanish genius—without doubt, the greatest painter ever produced in Spain—was also, in the opinion of many competent critics, the most incomparable painter of all time. There is a saying in Spain that to those God loves, He gives a home in Seville; and it was on June 5, 1599, that Velazquez was born in that beautiful city. His father was Juan Rodriguez de Silva; and Velazquez, the name by which he is famous all the world over, was that of his mother, Geromina Velazquez, a member of an ancient and noble family of Seville. His father, a cultured man, soon realised that his son was clever, and sent him to the university; but the boy was bent on an artistic career. It is doubtful whether his masters had much influence upon the young prodigy; the first of them, Francisco de Herrera, a man of violent temper, was so constantly at variance with him that they very soon parted ; and the young painter joined Francesco Pacheco, an artist of some ability and a man of considerable wisdom, who quickly realised the genius of his pupil and did his best to develop his great gifts in the right direction. So fond and proud did the old man become of his pupil that he approved, and perhaps suggested, his marriage with his only daughter, Juana de Miranda; and on April 23, 1618, Velazquez, being in his nineteenth year, the young couple were married, a union which proved a very happy one.

In 1623, Pachedo introduced his son-in-law to the all-powerful Comte Olivarez, through whom, after many attempts, Velazquez was brought to the notice of Philip IV, who commissioned him to paint his portrait, and so well pleased was he with it that he appointed him his Court painter with a studio in the palace. This important post, together with that of Master of Fêtes and Ceremonies, Velazquez retained for the rest of his life, though it does not appear to have been very remunerative.

The portrait of Philip IV, here reproduced, one of many such portraits, is considered by some authorities to be among the best half-dozen portraits in the world; in any case it is certainly one of the best in this country It

(*Continued*)

VENUS AND CUPID

By DIEGO DE SILVA Y VELAZQUEZ

In the National Gallery—Spanish School

was no small task to paint the somewhat gloomy and disappointed features of the Hapsburgh monarch, and to achieve a result full of dignity and magnificence; but it is what the great painter has done with consummate ease. The picture was formerly in the possession of Prince Demidoff, of Florence, and was acquired by the National Gallery in 1865 for a very moderate sum.

To the same period of his life belongs the magnificent " Venus and Cupid," also reproduced, which went by the name of " The Rokeby Venus," so called from its having been in the possession of the Morritt family at Rokeby. By the efforts of the National Art Collections Fund, which raised the sum of £45,000, this picture was presented to the nation.

In connection with this picture, it may be observed that representation of the nude by a Spanish painter of the period was extremely rare, owing to the austerity with which such studies were forbidden by the Church and the Court, and it was probably owing to the exceptional position of Velazquez, under the patronage of the King, that it was possible for this canvas to be painted.

In 1628, Velazquez had the good fortune to meet Rubens, his senior by more than twenty years, who was then in Spain on one of his diplomatic missions and who urged him to visit Italy, which he did shortly afterwards. In 1649, he paid a second visit to that country, where he painted the great portrait of Pope Innocent X. These visits were in all probability of the greatest value to Velazquez in the development of his native genius.

It may be remarked here that in most countries, especially the Italy of his day, painters were accustomed to live surrounded by coteries of friends and fellow-workers, much of which seem to have been denied to Velazquez in Madrid; it was probably the encouraging atmosphere he met with in Italy which contributed in no small degree to the production of his later masterpieces, for at home he was surrounded by the gloomiest traditions of an austere Court, a very trying climate, and, beyond the Court precincts, by a population quite indifferent to those artistic and literary ideals so dear to the Italian cities.

Like so many of the greatest painters, Velazquez produced a number of his best works during the last few years of his life, including " Las Meniñas " and others of his masterpieces in the Prado, at Madrid, which is the only

(Continued)

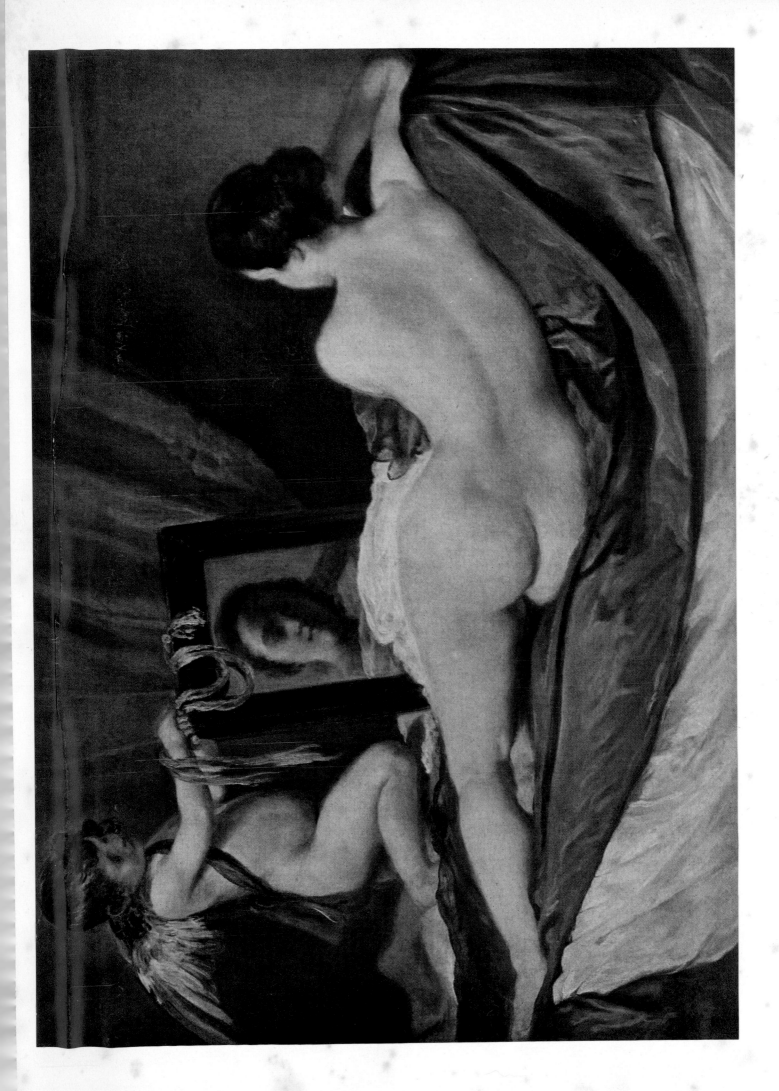

gallery possessing a really representative collection of the great Spanish artist's work. " Las Meniñas," or " The Maids of Honour," the third of our colour plates, is certainly one of Velazquez's supreme masterpieces; it was painted in 1655, five years before his death. It shows the small Infanta Margarita attended by her maids, who attempt to get her to sit for the artist, together with one of the odious little dwarfs which it was the nasty pleasure of the King to make the companion of his child. Velazquez himself appears on the left with his palette and brushes in hand. At the end of the room, reflected in the mirror, are Philip IV and his second wife, Mariana of Austria. A wonderful note in this picture, giving an idea of distance, is the open door through which a court official is passing. To artists, it is a matter of interest to learn from this picture the kind of brushes Velazquez used and also the setting of his palette.

It is sad to record that Velazquez, like many another artist of genius, was nearly always a poor man, in spite of his social surroundings, and that, almost immediately upon his death in 1660, a distraint was made on his possessions to reimburse one thousand ducats advanced to him by the authorities for some work in the Alcazar, unfinished at his death. Philip IV expressed much vexation at this, but did nothing to stop it. However, out of the sale sufficient money was raised to pay his debts and thus relieve his memory from any financial stigma.

On August 6, 1660, Velazquez died in Madrid at the age of 61. In the words of Señor de Beruete, " he surrendered to God the soul that He had created for the admiration of the world," and his wife and faithful companion, Juana de Pacheco, followed him to the grave a week later.

So ended a career which, in spite of all appearances, was marked by an isolation and indifference accompanied by a tragic struggle on the one hand with jealous enemies, and on the other against financial difficulties.

Velazquez was a genius who portrayed for us the life of Spain and, probably more than any other world-renowned painter, remained all his life quite unaffected by foreign painters, for he remained always entirely Spanish. To the Art which he wrought so brilliantly and to his devoted wife he dedicated his whole time regardless of material gains and left behind him a technique of painting which has been an inspiration to the present time.

Jan Vermeer of Delft
1632-1675

LITTLE is known of the personal history of this "Phœnix" who arose from the ashes of Carel Fabritius, his reputed master, the latter having perished in an explosion. A strange fate awaited this rare master. Though in his lifetime accounted great, for more than two centuries his fame suffered oblivion and, in the words of a recent biographer, "his works were shared out in various attributions among artists with more popular reputations." In recent times, a French critic resuscitated him; since when his fame, hand in hand with the market value of his pictures, has risen to a height and with a rapidity unprecedented in the annals of art.

Since his life was short and his methods were scrupulous to the last degree, his production was necessarily small. Less than fifty works are accounted to him. Born at Delft, in 1632, he married Catherine Bolnes in April, 1653, and, though he had a large family to support, he was never given to "pot boiling," but created his art slowly, for his masterpieces reveal hard work. Vermeer lived a regular, peaceful life, but suffered from lack of means in common with all the great Dutch masters; the bringing-up of ten children gave him little chance of thrift, and his daily struggle for a bare livelihood is a pathetic contrast to the joyfulness of his art. He has no rival in the employment of light and shade. Every object in the rooms he so loved to paint is bathed in a mellow glow; pure delight was granted to his brush. His repute was high among his contemporaries, and at the age of twenty-three he was elected president of the Guild of Painters of Delft. It seems that he never left his native country; in his earlier works, two of which contain nearly life-size figures, there are Italian influences, but these were quickly shed. His great reputation rests on his purely Dutch subject pictures, interiors and figures, one or two small heads of girls, and two faultless landscapes.

The National Gallery of London possesses one of the undisputed works by this great master, " Lady at a Spinet." Like all the work of Vermeer, this picture gives rise to no difficulty of appreciation; its beauty can be seen at

(Continued)

LADY AT A SPINET

By JAN VERMEER OF DELFT

In the National Gallery—Dutch School

Jan Vermeer of Delft
1632-1675

LITTLE is known of the personal history of this " Phœnix " who arose from the ashes of Carel Fabritius, his reputed master, the latter having perished in an explosion. A strange fate awaited this rare master. Though in his lifetime accounted great, for more than two centuries his fame suffered oblivion and, in the words of a recent biographer, " his works were shared out in various attributions among artists with more popular reputations." In recent times, a French critic resuscitated him; since when his fame, hand in hand with the market value of his pictures, has risen to a height and with a rapidity unprecedented in the annals of art.

Since his life was short and his methods were scrupulous to the last degree, his production was necessarily small. Less than fifty works are accounted to him. Born at Delft, in 1632, he married Catherine Bolnes in April, 1653, and, though he had a large family to support, he was never given to " pot boiling," but created his art slowly, for his masterpieces reveal hard work. Vermeer lived a regular, peaceful life, but suffered from lack of means in common with all the great Dutch masters; the bringing-up of ten children gave him little chance of thrift, and his daily struggle for a bare livelihood is a pathetic contrast to the joyfulness of his art. He has no rival in the employment of light and shade. Every object in the rooms he so loved to paint is bathed in a mellow glow; pure delight was granted to his brush. His repute was high among his contemporaries, and at the age of twenty-three he was elected president of the Guild of Painters of Delft. It seems that he never left his native country; in his earlier works, two of which contain nearly life-size figures, there are Italian influences, but these were quickly shed. His great reputation rests on his purely Dutch subject pictures, interiors and figures, one or two small heads of girls, and two faultless landscapes.

The National Gallery of London possesses one of the undisputed works by this great master, " Lady at a Spinet." Like all the work of Vermeer, this picture gives rise to no difficulty of appreciation; its beauty can be seen at

(Continued)

THE VIEW OF DELFT

By JAN VERMEER OF DELFT

In the Mauritshuis, The Hague—Dutch School

a glance and it may be said here that this is one of the infallible tests in considering great works of art.

One of Vermeer's chief merits is his innovation of daylight painting as opposed to chiaroscuro, or alternating light and shadow. Cool, illumined air pervades every corner of his finest canvases. They possess a crystalline clearness free from all trace of the brown sauce into which so many of his countrymen are wont to dip their brushes. In addition to his faultless workmanship, he was endowed with fastidious taste, a somewhat rare attribute among his contemporaries, and further he had a decorative sense unique amongst Hollanders. Hence, the high esteem in which his works are held to-day. Some idea of their preciousness, in terms of money, may be formed from the fact that the smaller of his two landscapes, the " Little Street " in the Rijks Museum, measuring only $21\frac{1}{4}$ inches by $17\frac{1}{4}$ inches, was purchased in 1921 for the City of Amsterdam by Sir Henry Deterding for no less a sum than £80,000. The landscape here illustrated, a view of Delft, is one of the glories of the Mauritshuis at The Hague. It shows the City of Delft bathed in the luminous air of a summer evening. Opposite are the Rotterdam Gate, with its flanking towers, and the Schiedam Gate, and between the two the water flows into the city. On the barge moored in the foreground, about which figures are grouped, may be seen Vermeer's signature, and near the centre of the picture traces of an additional figure are visible, which Vermeer, on second thoughts, painted out.

The enchanting little canvas " Portrait of a Young Girl " finds a place very near the top. Though it measured a bare $18\frac{1}{2}$ inches by 16 inches, its value in terms of money is inestimable. The great esteem in which Vermeer is held to-day dates only from 1866, when, after being neglected and forgotten for nearly two centuries, he was re-discovered by William Burger (Theophile Thoré), a French critic and collector. This writer made a list of seventy-two pictures attributable to this master, many of which have since been assigned elsewhere. To-day we are still something short of fifty undisputable works by this rare master, and the search for prizes still goes on.

Vermeer of Delft, this great creative genius, whose works are practically priceless to-day, died a poor man in his native town in his forty-third year.

MADAME VIGÉE LEBRUN AND HER DAUGHTER

By ELIZABETH LOUISE VIGÉE LEBRUN

In the Louvre—French School

Elizabeth Louise Vigée Lebrun
1755-1842

THIS " Mother and Child " picture, the most appealing of all pictorial subjects, is a never-failing attraction in the Louvre. That the painter was a beautiful woman is clear from this self portrait. In the picture she bears a strong resemblance to the well-known portraits of Madame Recamier painted by her contemporaries David and Gerard. By the former she was greatly admired both for her beauty and her talents.

Elizabeth Louise Vigée Lebrun was a born *Parisienne* and something of a coquette, though she did nothing to deserve the cruel treatment accorded to her by a heartless husband. She was the daughter of the painter Louis Vigée, from whom she received her earliest tuition. Better instruction came from Doyen, Greuze, and Joseph Vernet.

Her rise to reputation was extraordinary. By the time she was twenty she had become famous through her portraits of Count Orloff and the Duchess of Orléans, and was the idol of Society. Her life was filled with adventure. At twenty-one she secretly married J. B. P. Lebrun a painter and rascally art-dealer. Two years later, she was received as a member of the Academy on the strength of her picture " Peace bringing back Plenty." This picture hangs in the Louvre together with five portraits, in addition to two of her self and her daughter.

On the outbreak of the Revolution, Madame Vigée Lebrun fled to Italy. At Rome she painted the English princesses Adelaide and Victoria, and the self-portrait she had been invited to paint for the Uffizi Gallery in Florence; and, at Naples, her well-known " Lady Hamilton as a Bacchante," in the Tankerville-Chamberlayne collection. A triumphant tour through the capitals of Europe followed. Arriving in London, she took rooms in Maddox Street and here she painted the Prince of Wales—afterwards George IV— and Lord Byron. One of her most distinguished patrons was the ill-starred Marie-Antoinette, who loved her much, and of whom she painted no fewer than twenty portraits. In our National Gallery is a self-portrait of her in a large straw hat with her palette on her thumb. She died at the great age of 87.

FÊTE CHAMPÊTRE

By JEAN ANTOINE WATTEAU

In the National Gallery of Scotland, Edinburgh—French School.

Jean Antoine Watteau

1684-1721

IT is a strange fact that this short-lived genius of French Art was by blood a Fleming, although at the same time a French citizen from birth, as his native town of Valenciennes had been for seven years French territory. His father, Jean Philippe Watteau, was a Flemish carpenter.

The early talent of the lad caused him to cover every scrap of paper he could find with drawings so that his father, very unwillingly, sent him at fourteen to train with a painter called Gérin, with whom he stayed till his seventeenth year, when his master died. Owing to the complaints of Watteau's father that he was making no money, and his refusal to pay for further training, the sensitive young man fled to Paris, where, for many a day, he was to lead a life of extreme misery. There is no doubt that his sufferings from hunger and cold laid the foundation of the consumption which ultimately carried him off. In this state of penury he sought work in a picture factory near the river, where sketches were turned out by the dozen in return for a little food and less money.

In 1703, Watteau was fortunate enough to meet Claude Gillot, and with whom he painted many of his pictures connected with the theatre. From this period, his circumstances changed for the better and after some years, during which he studied and was influenced by the works of the old masters, he gradually developed a style of his own, full of grace, youth and elegance, with a delightful quality of broken colour ; he became the forerunner of the famous group of French Court Painters whose work he inspired and on whom he had a lasting influence. Watteau was the originator of the type of painting which might be called " Fêtes Pastorales," one of which, called by its French title, " Fête Champêtre," in the National Gallery of Scotland, we reproduce. Watteau was always restless, dissatisfied with his own achievement and never able to remain for long in any one place. His intense industry and lack of repose gradually wasted his remaining strength and after making arrangements for returning to his native home, he slowly sank and died on July 18, 1721, at the early age of thirty-seven.

HOPE

By GEORGE FREDERICK WATTS, O.M., R.A.

In the Tate Gallery—British School

George Frederick Watts, O.M., R.A.
1817-1904

A LIFE of selfless devotion to his art in continuous service to man-kind—such was the noble ideal Watts set himself and one to which he adhered till the end. To Watts, everything must have a purpose, must bear a lesson, be a message of hope, or serve as a beacon light to his fellow-men. Fortunately his gifts, as an artist, were equal to the burden imposed upon them. His technique, as a painter, he founded almost entirely on the principles and practice of the Venetian painters of the sixteenth century.

The son of a piano tuner of Hereford, Watts was born on February 25, 1817. He received little academic training, and from the first he followed an independent line of his own and became one of the foremost painters and sculptors of the nineteenth century. He took no interest in mere imitations or revivals of ancient art, but did his best to appeal to those of his own day, in spite of a tendency to moralise in paint, a habit peculiar to the time.

A prize of £300, which was awarded to him for his cartoon " Caractacus in Rome " for the decoration of Westminster Hall in 1843, enabled him to go to Italy, where he was taken under the wing of Lord Holland, British minister at Florence. Here he painted many portraits and executed a fresco for the Villa Carregi.

The picture, " Hope," which we illustrate, is probably one of the most poignant, as it is one of the most popular, of all the painter's work. It is pure allegory, the composition shorn of all accessory, simple as the idea. There is little left to hope for. Nothing remains to this pathetic, blind-folded figure, which yet retains its grace and its equilibrium in a circumstance of infinite desolation, save one frail string. The colour scheme of blue and bronze in subtle variations is particularly expressive and well calculated to give the utmost value to the painter's idea. The picture was painted in 1885 and first exhibited at the Grosvenor Gallery. It forms part of the great series generously bestowed upon the nation by the painter in 1897 now permanently housed in the Tate Gallery. He died at the age of 87.

"PORTRAIT OF MY MOTHER"
By JAMES A. McNEILL WHISTLER

In the Luxembourg, Paris—British School

James A. McNeill Whistler

1834-1903

ONE of the greatest artists of the nineteenth century at work in England was Whistler, who, like his friend Manet in Paris, was to lead a stormy life as a pioneer of new ideas so repugnant to the current Art of the time.

Born on July 11, 1834, at Lowell, Massachusetts, the son of Major George Washington Whistler, he was descended from an old English family and entered the West Point Military Academy at 17, but soon discovered his leanings towards an artistic life and, at the age of 20, he left America, to which he never returned. He went to study in Paris and was soon in the midst of the battle against the Salon (the French Academy) waged by Manet, Degas, Fantin-Latour, Monet and others. In 1859, at 25, he came to live in London and shared a studio for a time with Du Maurier, in Newman Street. Shortly after, he settled in Chelsea, in view of the Thames from which he drew his inspiration for so many studies of the river, studies with such a new vision that he was soon involved in London in the same artistic disputes he had known in Paris.

It is one of the strangest stories in the history of Art that it should have fallen to the lot of this American-born artist of genius to reveal to Londoners what their ancient river really looked like in certain aspects; and Whistler perhaps added to the hostility (as he generally did) by describing his pictures in musical terms, such as Nocturnes, Symphonies and so on, which, although singularly appropriate, made his critics still more furious.

To those of us who visit the Tate Gallery to-day and study that poetic masterpiece, "Old Battersea Bridge," painted in 1865, it will seem incredible that this lovely picture was one of the series which caused such bitterness, culminating in one of the most famous libel actions of recent times. It was in his thirty-eighth year that Whistler sent to the Royal Academy in 1872 his superb portrait of his mother which he called " Arrangement in grey and black," here reproduced, which the French Government purchased for the Luxembourg. Many a great artist has painted his mother—there is

(*Continued*)

"PORTRAIT OF MY MOTHER"
By JAMES A. McNEILL WHISTLER

In the Luxembourg, Paris—British School

James A. McNeill Whistler
1834-1903

ONE of the greatest artists of the nineteenth century at work in England was Whistler, who, like his friend Manet in Paris, was to lead a stormy life as a pioneer of new ideas so repugnant to the current Art of the time.

Born on July 11, 1834, at Lowell, Massachusetts, the son of Major George Washington Whistler, he was descended from an old English family and entered the West Point Military Academy at 17, but soon discovered his leanings towards an artistic life and, at the age of 20, he left America, to which he never returned. He went to study in Paris and was soon in the midst of the battle against the Salon (the French Academy) waged by Manet, Degas, Fantin-Latour, Monet and others. In 1859, at 25, he came to live in London and shared a studio for a time with Du Maurier, in Newman Street. Shortly after, he settled in Chelsea, in view of the Thames from which he drew his inspiration for so many studies of the river, studies with such a new vision that he was soon involved in London in the same artistic disputes he had known in Paris.

It is one of the strangest stories in the history of Art that it should have fallen to the lot of this American-born artist of genius to reveal to Londoners what their ancient river really looked like in certain aspects; and Whistler perhaps added to the hostility (as he generally did) by describing his pictures in musical terms, such as Nocturnes, Symphonies and so on, which, although singularly appropriate, made his critics still more furious.

To those of us who visit the Tate Gallery to-day and study that poetic masterpiece, "Old Battersea Bridge," painted in 1865, it will seem incredible that this lovely picture was one of the series which caused such bitterness, culminating in one of the most famous libel actions of recent times. It was in his thirty-eighth year that Whistler sent to the Royal Academy in 1872 his superb portrait of his mother which he called " Arrangement in grey and black," here reproduced, which the French Government purchased for the Luxembourg. Many a great artist has painted his mother—there is

(Continued)

a famous one by Rembrandt in the National Gallery, which is an incomparable study of old age, a very different type of woman, however, from the stately and aesthetic old lady who represents Whistler's mother. The artist himself felt, when exhibiting this work, that the public might not necessarily be interested in the fact that it was his mother, hence the first title was meant to draw attention particularly to the artistic qualities of the portrait. On the other hand, the reverent and tender treatment of this subject makes the human aspect of it very obvious. Certain it is that there are few such portraits of a mother painted by her son to be found anywhere.

Whistler was a man of strong combative instincts endowed with a witty, if somewhat bitter, tongue and it may be doubted whether he would in his own lifetime have secured the recognition he deserved had he not used these gifts in a persistent warfare against the powerful interests arrayed against him. His most memorable struggle was brought about by a fierce criticism of his work by the famous Oxford Professor of Fine Arts, John Ruskin. The enraged artist took action against Ruskin in the celebrated libel case, which opened on November 13, 1878, and resulted in Whistler receiving one farthing damages, Ruskin paying the costs. A public subscription being opened to defray these costs, Whistler magnanimously contributed the farthing granted to him.

About the same time that Whistler produced the portrait of his mother, he painted the magnificent portrait of Thomas Carlyle, which was purchased by the Glasgow Corporation Art Gallery from the artist, and it should be recorded to the credit of the Corporation that they were among the first of public authorities to recognise Whistler's genius, at a time when it was courageous to do so. If we have to admit that Whistler was, as a man, a quarrelsome little dandy, charming and insolent alternatively, quick to take offence and forever jeering at his own and his adopted countries, it must also be realised that he had many powerful and implacable enemies at a time when the practice of painting was at a low level. Always full of energy, he was an untiring worker at painting, etching and writing. This dapper little fighter, who though he had enemies, also cherished his friends, died in his 70th year in July, 1903, in his beloved Chelsea.

THOMAS CARLYLE

By JAMES A. McNEILL WHISTLER

In the Corporation Art Gallery, Glasgow—British School

a famous one by Rembrandt in the National Gallery, which is an incomparable study of old age, a very different type of woman, however, from the stately and aesthetic old lady who represents Whistler's mother. The artist himself felt, when exhibiting this work, that the public might not necessarily be interested in the fact that it was his mother, hence the first title was meant to draw attention particularly to the artistic qualities of the portrait. On the other hand, the reverent and tender treatment of this subject makes the human aspect of it very obvious. Certain it is that there are few such portraits of a mother painted by her son to be found anywhere.

Whistler was a man of strong combative instincts endowed with a witty, if somewhat bitter, tongue and it may be doubted whether he would in his own lifetime have secured the recognition he deserved had he not used these gifts in a persistent warfare against the powerful interests arrayed against him. His most memorable struggle was brought about by a fierce criticism of his work by the famous Oxford Professor of Fine Arts, John Ruskin. The enraged artist took action against Ruskin in the celebrated libel case, which opened on November 13, 1878, and resulted in Whistler receiving one farthing damages, Ruskin paying the costs. A public subscription being opened to defray these costs, Whistler magnanimously contributed the farthing granted to him.

About the same time that Whistler produced the portrait of his mother, he painted the magnificent portrait of Thomas Carlyle, which was purchased by the Glasgow Corporation Art Gallery from the artist, and it should be recorded to the credit of the Corporation that they were among the first of public authorities to recognise Whistler's genius, at a time when it was courageous to do so. If we have to admit that Whistler was, as a man, a quarrelsome little dandy, charming and insolent alternatively, quick to take offence and forever jeering at his own and his adopted countries, it must also be realised that he had many powerful and implacable enemies at a time when the practice of painting was at a low level. Always full of energy, he was an untiring worker at painting, etching and writing. This dapper little fighter, who though he had enemies, also cherished his friends, died in his 70th year in July, 1903, in his beloved Chelsea.

A CORNFIELD

By PETER DE WINT

In the Victoria and Albert Museum, South Kensington—British School

Peter De Wint
1784-1849

STUDENTS of Peter De Wint's work will not fail to detect in it a certain Dutch tranquillity and luminosity. He loved to paint wide skies and placid waters, and since he was of Dutch extraction his tastes for such aspects of Nature were probably hereditary, even though there is no known record of artistic talent in the family before him.

His father was a doctor who graduated at Leyden, finished his training at St. Thomas Hospital, London, and eventually set up as an apothecary at Stone, in Staffordshire, where Peter De Wint was born in 1784.

Intended for the medical profession, he managed to persuade his father to apprentice him to an artist, to wit, John Raphael Smith, the mezzotint engraver. De Wint also became a member of the Royal Academy schools, and before his studentship was over he was making a living by painting landscapes and teaching. He married the sister of William Hilton, his inseparable companion. While Hilton, who painted history and religion in the " grand manner," would have liked De Wint to follow his example, the latter concentrated on landscape work all his life, and was never happier than during the summer months when he was free to interpret Nature. The golden light on cornfields, large panoramas of fields with cattle, old houses and cathedrals were his chief source of inspiration. He painted both in oils and water-colours of which latter medium he is among the greatest of masters. In the words of John Clare, the poet, his work breathes " the living freshness of the open sky and sunshine, where the harmony of earth, air, and sky form such a happy unison of greens and greys that a flat bit of scenery on a few inches of paper appears so many miles away."

De Wint was fortunate not only in his art but in his domestic life, his wife being the best of helpmates. He lived within his means in the fullest sense of the word, never straining his genius beyond its capacity, gaining a modest living by the exercise of a unique sense of beauty.

De Wint died in 1849, and it was not until many years afterwards that his greatness was appreciated and his pictures began to realise high prices.

PRINCE ARTHUR AND HUBERT

By WILLIAM FREDERICK YEAMES, R.A.

In the City Art Gallery, Manchester—British School

William Frederick Yeames, R.A.
1835-1918

WILLIAM YEAMES has turned to English history, illustrating one of those episodes that have taken deep root in the heart of every English child. The fair-haired little prince in the picture is, with the two young princes murdered in the Tower at a later date, among their favourite heroes. No man knows the truth, but it is certain that the harrowing tale of Prince Arthur, Duke of Brittany and Hubert de Burgh owes most of its poignancy to Shakespeare's presentation of it. After being taken prisoner at Mirabel, and being escorted to Rouen, all trace of Arthur was lost. Be that as it may, history has saddled King John with a reputation of incredible villainy.

In the picture we see in the troubled face of Hubert the struggle between fear of his royal master and his own better conscience, further indicated in the tense gripping of his hands; the one clutching the table edge and the other clenched between his knees, whilst the appealing voice and looks of the child are obviously melting his heart to pity. Let us see how Shakespeare interprets the moment :—

" The scene is set in Northampton Castle. The boy has ' taken possession ' of his friend's heart, and reminds him that :—

When your head did ache

I knit my handkerchief about your brows

(The best I had, a princess wrought it me)

And I did never ask it you again ;

And with my hand at midnight held your head,

And, like the watchful minutes to the hour

Still and anon cheer'd up the heavy time,

Saying, " What lack you ? " and " Where lies your grief ? "

Or " What good love may I perform for you ? "

      . . . will you put out mine eyes ?

Hubert : *I have sworn to do it, And with hot irons must I burn them out.*

(*Continued*)

"WHEN DID YOU LAST SEE YOUR FATHER?"

By WILLIAM FREDERICK YEAMES, R.A.

In the Corporation Art Gallery, Liverpool—British School

Without, the executioners are waiting with heated irons, the cord to bind the victim is to hand. They enter. Yet the child's pleading prevails in the end. Rather than be guilty of " the foul corruption of a sweet child's death," Hubert relents, though it may cost him his own life. We can see that the artist has kept in mind Shakespeare's view of Hubert, whose rude exterior is " yet the cover of a fairer man."

In our second illustration, " When did you last see your Father? " the little patrician in his smart blue suit, true to his birth and breeding, stands up gallantly to his inquisitor. Perhaps he is aware that an unguarded admission may betray the whereabouts of the hiding Cavalier, whose portrait hangs before him on the wall above, and so bring disaster on his family. It was a time of sorrow in our land. In the struggle between King and Parliament it was inevitable that friends should be divided and that faction should breed hatred. Such an incident as the artist has depicted here must have taken place almost daily up and down the harassed country during the civil war, often with tragic consequences.

Cromwell's men have entered the mansion of one of King Charles's followers, obviously an active supporter and doubtless a man of importance. With the exception of the robust, fair-haired man in the light green tunic who sits at the table with his fists clenched before him, there is little leniency to be expected, judging by the grim expression of his associates. The house has been searched and ransacked. A large chest with a lid open lies upon the floor and a man enters the room carrying the owner's strong box. One of the sour-visaged Ironsides is about to press forward the weeping sister, scarcely older than her brother, in order to take her turn in the examination. The mother, an expression of tense anxiety clouding her proud features, stands back, her hand pressed to her bosom, in support of her daughter. So clearly has the artist told his tale that not an expressive detail is wanting.

This picture is one of Yeames's most important as well as one of his most popular works, the majority of which were derived from incidents in English history. He was born at Taganrog, in Russia, where his father was consul. After studying in Florence and London, he exhibited continuously at the Royal Academy, of which he became a full member in 1878. He was also librarian to the Royal Academy and curator of the Painted Hall, Greenwich.